Iliad Shattered

Also by the author

Mehen, the Oracle and the Time Movers

Iliad Shattered

Athena Gaga

KU
PRESS

A catalogue of this book is available from the British Library

ISBN 978 1 909362 65 9

Typeset in Bodoni 72
Cover and artwork by Rebecca Hampstead ©

Editorial and design by Kingston University MA Publishing students:
    Rachel Cotton
    Ida Langeland Hagen
    Rebecca Hampstead
    Priti Sundaram Mudaliar

KINGSTON UNIVERSITY PRESS
Kingston University
Penrhyn Road
Kingston-upon-Thames

KT1 2EE

Contents

Epoché

Kassandra's latent dream

Epoché

Kassandra's latent dream

Shadows of elemental and enigmatic affinities
(Setting in fire the clouds)
Tuned to light
(Renowned and ordained)

There is something that when it is spelled it rests nowhere
The moment is not always ready
(You never know for sure if it should be said)
It trembles in the line like a sound that has not yet found its place
(I wonder if I can and then again, I'm not sure)

But are places where their colour keeps waiting, getting ready
    to sink into the celestial bodies
No constellation has the patience to remove the night from the orbit
    of the day
The disc bounces on its reverse side
A dissolved frequency of abandoned materials

If it rained like yesterday, she would have changed her dwelling to
    the external but it rains like today and does not have the strength
    to leave.

She preferred conversations to silence
Arguments instead of words
And then with a flounder she shaped the waves
The first colour moored on the shore, the second went up, rolled
    over the highway, then changed course and turned back. The
    whole plot took place there.
Lost at isomeric intervals

We are not leaving tonight or tomorrow
The tree's branches tear pieces from the fading blue
(Vanishing inside)
The road erases the signs
Countless shadows, innumerable

Perhaps if we travel

But history as well as fairy tales have a beginning even if it is
  amorphous

These are the days when bitter misery pegs on figures and words

As if a tear transforms the whole face in a gaze of pain

The landscape; bites of sadness, air that stirs cold the spring

(The foliage cannot stand the icy sun)

Enclosed

Indifferent

Breathing has become a necessity and an occasion

Raise your head, shake off the dust from your hooves

Vigour

I translate the symmetry:

Saturn and Iapetus

Weary Clymene stands in the dark ocean. Gray salt and black stones
  mark the coastline.

Sweet vapour, white oestrus, holy sea

You forgot?

Delicate like fingers grabbed by the silence of a courageous body

Determined as the highest heavens

All my days stand as guides of Thryon

The sheaves tie forcefully the summer in sun bales

No fool would dare to cut the wild rose accidentally caught on the fence

Let it gush, source of earth colour, source of wood colour

One, two, three petals

Steps

One, two or three steps

The lever is fundamental in its size

I mean, it can resist the force exerted on it

I invoke its use

I guess as a distant resemblance

In order to describe the facts, I have to unnarrate them.

I mean it's not just the fantasy that anchors in delusion, sometimes
the prism lets us see the event itself as an illusion.

The trees

The lake

The balcony

Οι δε γε εγκαταλειπόμενοι[1]

The transfer of the field to the passage of a fuzzy operation

Example: from A to B the arrival is deleted precisely because it is not
framed

'Marching orders,' he said, and with a sharp look gave content to the
threat

Η χάρις εκπεπλήρωται[2]

For the second time, the victory is an amazing show

Ex post facto, there is no doubt
Ambiguous?
Rather majestic, maybe frosty
The proposal and the agreement did not offer the expected position

Memoir?
Correspondence?
Description?
I would say the key is in the process: it does not need to be
    disseminated that it can be restrained. (Exactly where it
    happens).

Inspired like a poem.
(Desire pierced his heart for the inspired girl)
She had candles lit in her room and a chair outside the door on the
    edge of the neighbourhood

I think she was wearing a shirt almost at knee-length
She had tightened it with a belt around her waist.
'Theatre tries to imitate life.'
'You think?'
'Yes, but I do not know if it succeeds.'
'People and their experiences?'
'Maybe, but I like simple affirmative sentences.'
'The theatrical structure as well as the theatrical space.'

'I'm bored,' she said. 'I just said something simply to say it.'

The imposing does not go unpunished

(Without peace perhaps)

Over time, even boldness can display weakness

The pariah instinct seizes the opportunity to evade

Access remains to the denial of all rights

(Purifying)

Assembling the resistance due to the lack of an alternative

Do not rely on certainty or balance

(Peacemakers)

Compensate for ignorance by believing in hesitation

For any reason, with any reason

The negligence

(Inevitably)

In the great Morning of the world (the definite article)

Outside the window the heat collects clouds of dust

The happy voice of an aloof moment

Guide to the concept or possibility of essence

Before the truth

(The roots)

Chance of apprehension

Semantic objects

(On incorrect presentation)
The art of the finite, rendering of the physical identity

I am so sorry that I am the subject of the poem
But how could it be otherwise?

Without the Eleatics
The experience of stress would have remained unsigned

Proximity
Search in the denials
Search in the rejection
Art is not the imitation of life

1 Those left behind, Herodotus, *The Histories*, Book 8.

2 The favour was fulfilled, *Herodotus*, The Histories, Book 9.

First

The atmosphere remained stable

Water, steam and greenhouse gases

(Albedo)

The moon is suffering

The *Roche* limit.

(Millions of microelements)

'I often wonder,' said Copernicus. 'If more logical positions of the
circles can be found.'

The rule of perfect movement

The one who was hiding was named Uranus

Souls, demons and Eumenides

The Titans devoured Dionysus

(The ashes contained the god)

Χρόνος αγήραος[1]
(Coincidentia oppositorum)
Κρούων νούς[2]
(Αήρ και Παρμενίδεια δόξα)[3]
Mystic frenzy or participation?

Repetition
Attendance comes first or maybe not?
Idealism, objectivity, intuition?
Absolute silence but not absolute inwardness
No issue.

Last night, in the snow, erotic attempt,
(Annihilation of the self)
The change of colours, the hidden companion
Violent freedom,
(Distance)
Quickly, before the contrast
Living nucleus
Dans une fleur rapide
Signe![4]
Start in a pleasant place (echoes in reflection)
Raison d'etre, desire of God

Πράξη, έργο, extensio
Receptacle *(Je n'ai pas lieu)*
Το των εικότων δόγμα[5]
Ανακυκλήσεις[6]
In the beyond?
In the infinity?
The precious product of a long chain of causes similar to one
    another.

Malbush
Moonlight, hidden springs, depth in invocation
Embroidered with beautiful stars
(Lustrous life, great in everything)
Blessed dancer
(The bliss given as a reward)
Sweet bells of heavens

Along the horizontal axis
Indefatigable fertility
But the earth is nothing but sand, the rocks of Mount Etna melt
    under the plow of the sun.

Cruelty is absurd
(Absurd and not lawful)
Outrageous and not necessary

Long blond hair, scented

Messenger's warranty, pledge of oracle

(No antinomy)

Automaton or living organism? Not enough attention is paid to the
definition

To strengthen, to endorse or to associate?

(The insufficiency of the factors of production does not matter)

Calm order

Pure fact

Tua res agitur

Let's not rush

Sober

Rely exclusively on the selective fact. Quality of devotion. Mixed
blessing.

Usurpation?

The nature, the miracle, the uncertainty.

(Overt)

Likely or unlikely?

Creative material

From the point of view of science, I can say that I share the delusion.
Perhaps the error is equal to the sum of the cases or the loss of
those who are abandoned.

Procedure of doubt.

(Imagination in the remembrance)

Insurmountable, consistent and selfish distrust

Steps in reverse direction

Renewed celebration of the woodlands and the open pastures

The hand of Hippodamia or the passion of Oenomaus?

The authentic road is accidental.

1 Ageless time.

2 Nous that blasts elements against each other.

3 Air and Parmenidean doxa (the Way of Appearance/Opinion).

4 Reference: Stéphane Mallarmé, *Poésies*, 1887.

5 In all probability, apparently.

6 Events take a cyclical course and happen again.

Second

Sea urchins

Underwater forests

The surface begins to freeze

(The difference between winning or losing)

Lines of Demarcation

Giant waves travel along the coastline

Explode with life, disturbance of seawaters, planktonic creatures

Oxygen

(Abundance)

> Oh, my little transparent shell the rosy dawn's sweet
> ornament

Undisputed obligations

(Pure self-defence)

Heretic

Free from each other, dark figures

Unexplored Atreides, seal of threat

I watch the river that crosses the mountains

Award

Magnificence

Brilliantly revealed

Eurydice: *Toujour aimer, toujour souffrir, toujour mourir*

Triumph or the plot's convention?

The playwright is not interested in a happy finale

Ominous radiation

Lightning, thunderstorms, action

Disasters

Sudden reconciliation

(Light flickers in front-facing mirrors)

Alcmene meets Phaedra

(But she doubts if she should)

Dual power or a completely personal image of the world glowing
    with the rhythm of the strange hour

Excellence and Harmonisation

Fine processing

Destiny

(The deep waters of conjecture)

Shiver and vision

Light aura, a sunset, the ethereal beauty

We had a pine tree in our garden

(The happiness of a child, the sweetest of all)

Smile of old sadness

'Open the window'

Smell of summer

Obvious

Gift and dreaming

Diodorus said: *il fut tue par Hecatée*

Diodurus said: *Par dela le fleuve des confins du monde*

Une mer interieure, faire de la magie, lire dans les astres

Consciousness is a desired experience and it obviously has content.

Third

Detector

(Gravitational effect)

Particle interactions

The colourless alternates with rusty red, an ancient desert

(Sediment from evening light)

Accumulation of events: a sunbeam confronts the question,
    wandering spins in the past

(Hidden, in the public view)

Is the price worth it or not?

Phoenician ship in a breeze

(Hospitable affection, in a foreign country)

Dark poplar and amber-coloured soil

Brave prize; exquisite jewellery sculpted by clouds and dense mist
Fair wind
Ropes and helmsman touch the blue

Pain and bitterness in her eyes
But his hands are encouragement, warm heart and love
Floating over her, seeing only her eyes
(Turning aesthetics into ideology)
The lizard is resting in the shade
(The grace of nature or naturalness)

'How long does it take to get to your destination?'
'*Un état d'âme musical.*'
'To discover the conditions of life?'
'Quotations.'
'To integrate memory into the poetic experience?'
'Assign a mission: recall the time of empty spaces and fair winds.'

The fabric is torn and crumpled
(Symbols of power or error)
Fragments of knowledge
(Taunt)

Lunar eclipse, days before the final attack
The wind is changing.

Repulsion

Time's deposits; mental durations
Confessing: compensation
Wavy conception, perhaps secondarily called intuition
(The speaking oaks)

Aeschylus said: word may heal word
Aeschylus said: not violence but cunning gives victory
Guiding idea: directorial presentation, power claim
Variable geometry: shade of inspiration

The enigma, a worn-out hypothesis, suggests the poem's ability to
produce silence. And, perhaps, a throbbing sense of infinity.

Fourth

Exploration

(Basaltic field)

Excavation

(Life ingredients)

Pushing

(Metal hydrogen; collectors)

Folding

(A specific red, almost burgundy, and a specific green, almost
    almond)

A wicker chair; a landmark

(Indication of my peculiarity and perhaps my mood)

Words liberate memories: organic regulation, galvanic reaction,
   phonological composition.
(Additional note: intersection of projection and identification)
I tried to touch them: a peach; the coolness of the night
Sense: *alfresco*
(Sudden transition to the dream)
The story unfolds in successive readings
Temples, amphitheatres, columns
(Free, however charged in the landscape)
Cracks, functions, bonds
(Intentionally inaccessible)
Interpreter
(Faint breathing)
The dry, soft surface evokes the intoxication of acceptance
(Black steam, one with ether)
Shrubs and bushes
(Mournful glint)
The other point of view
(Mental reasoning, patterns, comparative loans: genealogy)
Successive additions
tu nos fecisti ad te
απόρροιαι [1]

Mythical; namely genuine.
Belief; in the light of the reconstruction of the elements, a single

historical place.

(Primary break-in)

Psychological balance: fall and reintegration.

Social imprint: recorded in the human body.

Habitus: the holders of legality.

Liminality: the exclusive relationship between events is almost
always a matter of chance.

The pond, divided into an eastern and western area by a bridge, can
easily deceive eyes; our reflections function as motives.

Space belongs to appearance.

1 Reverberations.

Fifth

Mapping

(Alpine meadows)

Spectacular outcome

(Crossroads. Poles are extinguished. New approach.)

Iconographic wording, intricate game of perspective.

Gentle beauty, accentuated shading, weighting, awareness, mission.

(Preface to intense activity)

Erotic fragment: Abandoned, unnatural flowers and imaginary
     beings.

Πτεροφυές or the feather shafts swell and rush to grow from their roots:[1]

Clear outline, inconceivable, and perhaps, inexplicable outcome.

Instantanés:
Your gaze.
(I love you)
Your gaze.
(So should I leave?)

Grumpy lyre, hit of luck.
Ενώπιον του βήματος του χρόνου:[2] *Je ne sais quelle profonde*
    tristesse habitait mon âme.[3]

Immersion,
We wanted the wonderful; breath from an unknown life.
And then, all were placed in the titles of the spectacle.
(Exquisite mood made of enamel and gold)
Evening light on the window

Desire: ancient music
Victim of my misconception or of your untimely kindness?
Frightful waiting in my soul

Foam made from cringed waves
Hope made from hurling rocks
Swirling (Distillate)

Scaled:

Books, blank papers, empty files

(An extremely complex analysis of experiences)

The magical energy of natural things

(Τα συμβεβηκότα)[4]

The center of oscillation, manifestation of fluid matter.

(Vulnerable to your appealing)

Tancredi in Syracuse

Maroon gown, laurel wreath: Triumph

(Select a template)

'What a disaster,' shouted the prophetesses Fimonoi.

'*Chrysoneiro*[5] I see you because the water in the cold spring has
    enchanted me'[6]

(The poet's shadow on a stone table and around span high
    mountains)

Κύρου πεδίον: Θρυαλλίς[7]

Intoxicating scent, sent from the depths of the world, *ίαμα*

Preservation,

Monuments, heirlooms, olive groves, mulberries, fruit trees

Bloom,

Moist soil, abundance.

Engraved,

ʿανάσχουσα τας χείρας,'[8]

Unpretentious, wonderful,

Embossed model,

Female bust, noticeable resemblance, proportion,

Reason,

The colour, volume and shape of personal emotion

(Propeller from a black ship)

Eclectic performance or escape element

Frosted time,

(Its branches are very dense and lean towards the ground)

Between the 45th and 67th southern parallels with a deviation and
between the hours of 16 and 30 minutes and the 18th, correct
reference: Thirty-seven stars, a primordial ocean, granites,
decaying matter and steady growth.

A challenge is set to the imagination's capacity; we will discover the
nexus or perhaps we will discover the existence of the essential
being.

The ambivalent emotion, at the moment, pleases me.

1 Reference: Plato, *Phaedrus*.

2 In front of the time's throne.

3 Reference: Jean-Paul Sartre, *Nausea / La nausée* -1938.

4 The praedicamenta (Aristotle).

5 (latinised Greek) Golden Dream.

6 Reference: Lorentzos Mavilis, *Sonnets*, 1910.

7 Battle of Corupedium/ the plain of Kyros : wick/cause that triggers an event.

8 Raising her hands.

Sixth

The mountain,

(Impenetrable barrier)

At the southern end, smooth zone, mines

The first settlers, a strange but happy coincidence

(Shellfish, in absolute order, in the middle a cylindrical appendix as
    well as a boxed amount of air so that they can float in the water,
    from a distance look like a blue egg with a grey spot)

Headstone:

(αι Ταναγραίαι κόραι)[1]

Secret and deep ray of love

Sacred spring, Aganippi
(επί του Ελικώνα)[2]

With the first division, negotiations
(But also, fortifications on the north side)

Calligraphy:
In Gadeira or in Jutland
(The promise along with the hope)

Heroic figures, forthcoming, thyrsus from a vine branch
(Gentle passion)
Butterflies and other beautiful insects and flowers
(Orchids and maybe irises)
Increasing influence
(Paean)
Instinctive crude expression
The cranes of Ibycus, black-veiled Eumenides

Anxiety.
Speech that mediates.
(The mediator disappears within it)

Under the cinder of the dead fossils
(Citadel with high tower, sloping level and retaining walls)

The island is oval in shape, with secluded beaches and solitary suns.

Leaning on the wooden desk he looks at the door.

(High collar, wide sleeves, gold chain, all out of tune with the
    contextual)

Who has installed him there?

She approaches, opens the drawer and closes him inside.

Alignment: the ease of a straight line.

Habit: not to be interested.

Mention: to leave without hesitation

I'm glad we stayed friends anything else would have been annoying

(I wanted to say boring)

Maybe I'm scared, I do not know, it seems so difficult

C'est le reflet de mon visage: Je ne me sens seul quand je suis seul.

I really do not want to be rude

(I prefer to take the responsibility for the failure)

Spiritus lenis

Γλυκεία μοι μήτερ[3]

(Shadow and flutter)

Memory

(The invisible, the blessed, the eternal)

The slope, inaccessible
(Stalagmites)

Dull days, salty light, shipwrecked
(Breath of a wounded animal)

Daybreak of the night; silk on Melpomene's shoulders
(Silvery highlights, milky white, light blue)
Sky image.

The form, product of selected recovery. A quick look at the text
reveals the sequence of expressions. Quality transfer. Active
mood. Arrogance of belief.
Captivated by inclination and appetite.
Supposition: The vital force, self-maintaining, animating,
aggregating into magnitude and quantity, attracted while
repelled, delightful, realised in acts, embellishing the aspect of
judgement as the state of comprehension.

1 Tanagra figurines.

2 On the mount of Helicon.

3 My sweet mother.

Seventh

Divine *νάμα*[1]

(To embrace you lest I erase my sorrow)

Flower garden

(Kotinos:[2] victory's wreath)

The winged goddess placed on the right palm

(Nice monument, sloping on the pebbles)

Internal event:

Experience and interpretation

Fatal and unavoidable

(New and original associations)

Two hours before dawn, swimming in the fog, the night brought
    peace
(Purple roses)

Cave:
Art hidden in nature, raw rocks and minerals,
(Complex of veins and nerve bundles)

When Iamos heard the cheers of the generals, he assured his mother
    that the number and type of harmonics that accompany the
    fundamental sound, in fact, is like a wave. The wave does not
    move only its shape changes.

Multi-syllable echo,
(Clash of wills)

Corymb,
(Apex)
Search for the bodily image; the experience of other souls

That smile,
(Carefree, small flute, sweet crimson).

Attraction,

(Shooting stars in parabolic orbit, revolving)
And then,
(The narration stopped)
Simple transfer of biological characteristics.

Reminder:
Attention gentlemen,
Caution

From one sea to another
(Laurels, thyme and resin)
Hewed stone, fleeting impression
(Sleepless castle in the wilderness)

Child standing on a dolphin
(Cloud that looks like violet droplets)
Its beauty overwhelms you

They were laughing or felt melancholic
(Courtesy, deep cyan silence, bright alabaster moons)
Too enthusiastic descriptions?

The warm rays of the sun
(Waters as calm as oil),
Holy wish

(Pearl tear),

Heavenly moment

(Pulse and caress)

Inexhaustible horizon,

(Wings of a dream in the dim)

Pulsed state inspired by emotion

(Stamens and pistils, deciduous plants and flowers, elliptical leaves
fluffy like feathers, are assembled on the firmament with the help
of the wind alone)

Lush Grapevine

(Ad infinitum)

The coming generations.

1 Spring water.

2 (Latinised Greek) olive wreath.

Assembled

Iliad's women

Swayed

Aegialia

I married Diogenes

We settled down in a fine wealthy house

He excelled all Argives

The self-control: my quality

A cherished wife

Shed tears?

We all know: The man who fights the gods does not live long.

The fields were dark

Full with trooping ghosts

Uncertain allegiance to an alternate sway

Night after night. Deep loneliness.

Ilium

Iron hue

The son of Tydeus

Within my eyes

Sunken eyes

Expiring glances

Is this fidelity?

From place to place.

And me?

Settled down by myself.

I decided to keep the horse, my grandfather's horse, Areion.

Thus, I kept the horse, the house and all the securing resources:
    assets and power.

The traditional approach.

Areion an object of affection?

I will say,

Preferably,

A preference.

Areion can be equally benevolent to anyone

Appeased

Aethra

Shades of ancient worlds
A return, a continuation, a temporal window
The nature of nature

Over me
(In the salt green depths)
An almond tree
My story or my grandson's story
It doesn't matter
It is the same
Gifts to warm my heart

Gifts to beat off that disaster

Look! The great city burning
A black cloud
This phenomenon belies the realist's view
A moral opprobrium
Highly loaded with meaning,
In other words: 'infused with value'
Perhaps awaiting an alternative explanation
Phyllis's death in a new context
What has been looked upon was a prohibition
In the ensuing years
Supplementary pressures, domestic evolution, rival visions
Phyllis and Macaria: isomorphism.
As a grandmother I have to say that manipulating the self-
    presentation might have a double effect and a double
    hermeneutic.
Somebody might speak for the swarming tribalism and another for
    the fluidity of the postmodernism in the contingency plane versus
    agency plane.
My argument, as a grandmother, is simple:
My grandson has done exactly what he had to do. He transcended
    time and space.
After all, in the heart of the story there is a geographic diffusion of
    both description and explanation.

48

I, the mother of Theseus, belonged in the servitude of Helen.

Thus Demophon, my grandson, must perceived as my wilful gestalt
over my choice.

Appease or disagree, it is a central element illuminating my idea of
the self as an evolving image: modified, projected, displayed,
incarnated and articulated furiously blowing across fate's trench.

Reversed

Agamede

Child, please don't cry,
Let me add and stir a tale about the ancient witch's day

Gone to the garden,
She strokes the rock.
Watching the dark,
Her frenzy fires up,
She chants, she spells and transforms
The evil eye has gone

Bringing the moon down to the earth

Rain and storm move in the front
Enemies and friends stay still
Fair weather appears firm
She chants, she spells and transforms
The evil eye has gone

Simulatrix, piatrix, expiatrix, cantatrix
Never again a *strix*
You must know though, my sweet child:
The ancient witch has never died.

She chants, she spells and transforms
Locking an entire city indoors,
She chants, she spells and transforms
Throwing a man's home to a barren mountain dome
She chants, she spells and transforms
Casts her shadow upon all
She gets the rays behind her
A binding spell of purified strength
The incantation's trance
Speech acts upon the soul's nuance
Purifiers, mages and charlatans
Will never control the ancient witch's unfathomed lands
The inherent power of her words
Her influence on the external world

Pharmakis, Hiereia or Mantis

Her amulets bewitch your eyes bliss

Magical remedy, reversed expectation, relief of pain

Such flamboyant gifts to win your praise

Shearing and carding,

Spinning and weaving

knitting and toiling,

The ancient witch chants her spells and adorns your life

The stars light

A summer night

Remember child,

The ancient witch will always be by your side.

(Your sweet dreams will bring your love and your love will dance
    every dance with you for the rest of his life)

Transited

Alcestis

Wait and hear: 'If only your ghost might come back and delight me
in my dreams.'[1]
Wait and hear: 'I am so little, Father, and lonely and cold.'[2]

Statuesque: silent and veiled. Wrapped in mist.
Detached: mallows and asphodels. Anointed for Thanatos. Empty of
hopes.
Obscured: black Death and chilled Hades. Weaving of the varied
web. Blackened threads.

Wait and hear: 'The chirping grass-hopper sits in a tree and pours
down his shrill song.'[3]

And now, pray: deep-blue spring, dance on soft feet.
And now, accept: black fate, the murky Night clothed in dark clouds.
And now, see: the clarity of the day, the sun. Vivant.

Rite de passage?
The allusion of a new geography?
The mythic archetype. Heracles. Saved me.
Dust and time dissolved under the robust light in my blood. Alive.

(I have nothing to say about my husband. It seems as I was never
married to him. You see, he loved dummies or the ideal femme,
as he was claiming. He called himself a romantic. Heracles
was so funny. He made me laugh. I was delighted. Sometimes
he enjoyed role play. He was Orpheus and I was Eurydice.
Searching for me all over the place. The place was the beautiful
alleys of Iolcus. He constructed a pavilion just for me. We met in
secrecy. I told you. Was fun. My marriage was vacant. A bad joke.
Thus, we devised a fair prank. Cruel perhaps. Yes, I admit so.
But I was tired of my husband's selfish romanticism or whatever it
is called. My practicality. Out of boredom. I had to do something.
The ruse of a desperate housewife. That was all. Harmless, I
think. At the end of the day, we all got what we wished for).

1 Reference: Euripides, *Alcestis*.

2 Reference: Euripides, *Alcestis*.

3 Reference: Plato, *Phaedrus*.

Conceptualised

Alcmena

We construct the world, each time we look upon it
This particular arrangement ceases to exist when we turn our eyes

The mother of Heracles, the queen of Thebes
Just one reference, a comparison
A remote and distant passion

Alcmena woke up in her true self
(Under the blue waters)
(Over the dazzling skies)
As she appeared in her mirror

(A psychic function of reconfiguration

A departure

And at the same time a trajectory

Denominating the stars or perhaps desired as a naturally existent
     claim)

Zeus pondering contemplation

Conceptualised as a central pivot: the hero to come.

Heracles

Despite the fact that the inventory, the centric conglomeration of a
     potency,

Was about Life

Alcmena was abandoned

while Zeus's multifaced arena encircled the oceans in his
     primitive authenticity

Lulled

Andromache

I was walking near a beautiful tree,

A Sycamore

There was a spring of clean water

Small flowers and grass

My son played

We played

Together

The Sycamore had dark green leaves

Little birds, tiny voices

I sang something about the birds and the tree and the yellow honey
bees

My child was smiling
My husband
We loved each other, we loved our son, our world

Now I have another son
Bearing the fields, bearing the need
I never stopped lamenting my son
I am alive for my son

There is a place not too far from my new home
A Sycamore tree,
A spring with clean water,
My child smiling
My son
The sky glows as if nothing happened
The past never existed
Nothing to weep upon
Tender love
Calm delight
Gentle little birds
A beautiful sound
Warmth lulls in the soft air
Bathing in my son's eyes
Such a pure light
Bees and birds and far away clouds

Cradling my sweet treasure, innocent hope

My thoughts are silent, soft moths

Soft fingers touching mine

How strange

Fragile wildflowers spreading their fragrant sweeping away the shoving woes

Breathing love untroubled from worries

Inhabited

Antaea

'No man exists who is fortunate in every respect.'[1]

A moralising maxim. Free-floating. Nothing to do with me. I
    assure you.

Raising of the curtain: 'I give to you praise to the height of the
    sky, and I kiss the earth to the width of the earth.'

You must have known that my name was Stheneboea, I was the
    cattle queen.

A lady of charm. A magical, fertile, seductive mother. The
    archaic maternal matrix. Nourisher and seducer.

That I was.

I was not a woman in a doorway. Nor a failed residue of

passion. My bovine form reaffirms the fluidity of meaning. A numinous primordial mother, inhabited by animated entities.

That I was.

Bellerophon. The killer of his brother. Fratricide leading to a series of enactments: the killer of the cattle queen. The killer of prehistoric darkness. Heritage of a forced acculturation.

The ancient holiness of the cattle, a static surface, a self-contained message.

Melampus. Killed an ox and talked to the vultures. The cattle, my daughters, were spiral-horned and broad of brow. He trapped them in the Cave of the Lakes, feeding them hellebore roots.

Melampus. Deception, abduction, and murder was the trajectory of Bellerophon's narrative. He was able to change their psychic and physical form. Perhaps that was part of the recurring cosmogonic act. While Bellerophon's pure breaching created a vestige of a poisonous triangular relationship. Passions raged.

Thus, I became an explicit model for women's suicide. An ungraspable primal repression. I am both living and inert. Since then, the instinct is denied entrance into the conscious. You see every new association modifies and reveals possibilities that may seem insuperable. But there are always traces of previous strata that has been erased so

that new strata can take place: The atavism of primaeval
times.

I tried to translate my raw emotion into love-object.
Bellerophon denied my offer haunted by his radical
reasoning. This is how I became a buried memory.
Censored, transmuted and discarded.

1 Reference: Euripides, *Stheneboea*.

Embedded

Ariadne

(Minotaur, or the eternal enigmas of duality and paradox)
What you see depends on where you stand, I was never
*   embedded in the labyrinth.*

My brother. His face. His head. Mutated. My father said that he was
a disgrace. The Great Priestess, my mother, persuaded him not
to kill the baby. 'The gods will not approve his death.' He agreed.
Poor creature. I was not allowed to approach him. I wished to
approach him. I was just a little girl. I loved my poor brother.
I was not allowed to speak to him. I was not allowed to touch
him. I was only allowed to sit opposite him and stare at him. The

labyrinth. A prison. Was not made for my brother. It was used long ago. Enemies died there from starvation not being able to find their way out. They were given the chance but not the means. They were told that they will enjoy freedom if they were able to find the path to freedom. Such a lie. Daedalus made sure that no one will be able to find the circle that led out. There, in this prison, they have abandoned my brother. He was so little. Deserted and lonely. I went every day to visit him keeping in my hands my way out; my ball of thread. My father treated him like an animal. Feeding him like his wild dogs. He never allowed my mother to see her son. I went every day. We looked at each other. I knew that he recognised me. In the room's dim light, our eyes met, conversing the intense monotony of the huge stone blocks laid in double courses. My brother was a prisoner. Sometimes I wished to entertain him. I jumped up and down or I was taking steps back and forth as if I was dancing and he was imitating me. I smiled. He laughed. He knew how to laugh. Then he looked so human. So really human. More human than anyone I knew. My father found out. He brought this strange device. A red mask. He attached the mask on my brother's face and head. My brother was obliged to wear constantly this terrible thing. I was banned from ever visiting him again. I never again saw his smile. I never again heard him laugh. But I was sneaking inside the maze without my father's approval and I was sitting next to him. As he grew older, he behaved more and more like an animal. My father, I suppose.

His treatment. He ate raw meat like wild beasts do. I could see his eyes through the mask. I couldn't see his mouth. It was covered, apart from when he ate. Then my father adjusted the horns. Bull's horns. He taught him how to wrestle. How to box and hunt. He had to chase small animals to eat and finally he had to slaughter humans. Still, I used my thread to visit him every single day. He was a young man when Theseus passed the crenellated gate. A single arched doorway, followed by a multiplicity of detours. Daedalus filled those countless paths with confusion. Wove them with blind walls and deception. Odd repetitions. Irretraceable wanderings. Reversals and gaps. But I was there leading him. Step by step. Room after room. Corridor after corridor. This construction had no guardians. No need. Getting in was a death wish for anyone except me and my father. Inevitable to get out. I made up my mind only few days ago. I visited my brother. I saw his eyes full of tears. He chained him. Then unleashed him only to devour his enemies. We looked at each other. He closed his eyes. Something dreadful must have happened. I saw blood coming out of his neck. The mask. Something with the mask. It looked like it was now not an attached device anymore, but part of his face and head. I gave Theseus my sword. My brother kneeled. Theseus beheaded him. In one hit. Then we attempt to take the mask off. Release his face. We couldn't. As I thought, it had become one with his skin. In our struggle we broke one horn. That was all. My father was a monster. I begged Theseus to let me in Dia. All the tears that were amassed inside me for so many years spread out like a furious river. I fell asleep but Theseus kept his promise. There was me, the most holy, the utterly pure, the Mistress of the Labyrinth, in a dry island, in the middle of the sea. Sleeping under a lonely tree. Sleeping while a gentle wind wrapped me as with a fine linen shroud. In my dream my brother came. He was wearing a golden kilt around his loins and a deerskin on his shoulders. He kept a floral crown in his hands. A crown for me. When I looked upon his face, the red mask was there. But then, his eyes were laughing. Instead of the bull-horns sun rays spread a halo of light around his head. He was handsome like a new-born god. Suddenly I found myself in the middle of a bullring or an arena while the blue-masked jeering crowd was reduced to monstrous hunters and devourers of my magnificently gilded brother. A strange feeling as if I was submerged in water. Blue streams, black turns, red mosses. I was gliding. In dual flows. I flew back. Again. And again. My flower crown turned into a constellation of stars. Isolating the moment. The entropy of the unguarded centre, understood as a dream or reflection. A hybrid monster, a repetitive and melancholic self, located in the centre. A snail, a spiral-shaped shell in a vertical placement. A single, immobile point. Advanced and retreated. The labyrinthic architecture of the space was collapsing into one dimension. There was no escape. I was locked in. The pride of Minos, the lust of Pasiphae, the cleverness of Daedalus, the tragedy of Icarus, the love of Ariadne, the horror of the Minotaur, and the heroism of Theseus. All were fitted in a pattern. Static without possibilities. On the top of a powerful pyramidal rock Theseus wearing a phylactery on a red-brown cord around his neck jumped up and roared in a terrible voice. The unwelcome recurrence of the nihilistic past: Theseus's rash nature. My soul stretched out. A moment of perfect joy. 'Bacchus loves flowers,' my brother said. My earthly life, my diadem, formed the Corona Borealis while I was hanged from the tree.

Associated

Astyochea

A gold vine for a son, a family heirloom in exchange for a male
    offspring.
That was my sacrifice for Scione.
They, who set fire to the ships, wrestling with the future, activated
    a picture of the future (actions and their qualities: an ever-
    changing illusion)
My son, defending Troy.
My husband, on the pattern of the past, healed by Achilles.

'Thinking or imagining, feeling and willing.' The key is lost.

A dream figure consisting of conflicting currents: the
   unconscious dimension of my being.

An original intuition: without breaking the image, I saw
   my house invaded by a horse. The symbol-horse. A
   gigantic cryptogram. The active impression. An opening.
   Participating in my actuality, Troy reveals a supersensible
   reality.

Autumn.

Translucent. Broad. Distinctive.

Green carriers of a truth: leaves that grow self-oriented.
   Converging, fusing idea and experience. Codified as
   uninterrupted series of transitional cases. In this sense,
   while the ships were floating in the sea far from the Misyan
   lands, blue seemed to retire from my psyche. The mystery
   of accessing myself was profoundly deep. Almost as a
   ressentiment altered to a reactive challenge in front of an
   opportunity. Blue argued no more within my heart. Both, we
   belonged to a newly situated association. The city to come.

Climbed

(Astyoche)

I am so frightened. I am afraid of living alone.

I am afraid of loneliness.

The house turns into a scary, empty and remote space.

How can I inhabit such space?

We are not made for loneliness.

It was better at my father's place. Why did I leave? Why did he let me
    leave?

Such a bad idea. To live far from my beloved home.

(I did not wish to live alone anymore.)

I was drawn into melancholy and fear.

(Mother. Father. I miss you. Please let me back in.)

My heart was shrinking in her privacy. Feeble and perplexed.
Narrowed and blocked. Sensitive and distressed. Strained and
tensed. Vanishing and mangling into my crushed nerves.

I don't know where I found the courage. It was pitch dark when
I climbed into the upper rooms and fell into Ares' arms.
Deep inside I knew that was the only way out of my sorrow
and fears.

Ares immediately felt my need. He shared his strength with
me.

I had two wonderful sons. I never again felt lonely and
powerless.

Raped

Briseis

The rage goddess turns the tide, united
So many souls, warm embrace.
Begin, Muse, begin
Respect my daughters, respect my sons, respect the wounded shrill
of cry

Inhuman
The second wind bursting across, charged in full force
The raw pain, flesh racked with pain, trembling fire, wrapped in full
pride

'Disgraced and shameless man,' Briseis voice commands the fight.
'Damned Atrides. My silent tears drown in your pitiless heart.
My Nemesis's warrior: Clytemnestra, a woman like me.'[1]

'I wished her free. Not my trophy. My powerful wife.'
'I wished her free.'
Achilles warned them.
'Achaeans, do not fear the abuser's rotten heart.'
Achilles warned them.
Did they listen?
Let us hear.

With the contagion of a mother's hate, he met his own image;
    Iphigeneia was revenged

Free outspokenness, immediate significance, strength
The angels of justice, *le grand tout*, the truth
A call to remembrance, the moral law of duty and right

Achilles warned them
Did they listen?

I ought to be free, for existence is not an object neither a division
I ought to have knowledge of my being
I ought to have my own determination

I ought to have a predicate identical to myself

The content of truth it is not an intellectual knowledge, it is
    justice
The Rage-Goddess, my mother, warned them
Did they listen?

Briseis, the bearer of the quiver
The unreconciled wrath
Did they listen?

Rage-Goddess, Me Too I was raped
Listen to me
I demand Justice

1 Reference: Iphigenia in Aulis, Euripides.

Self-Reflected

Kassandra

When I try to rest, melancholy slithers inside me

Concerns tied to contradiction

Rejected or accepted: a binary self-modified boundary

Me, the unresolved subject

Deep in peace crocus and hyacinth, the holy earth bursts, a rippling
stream

The grip of numbness, waves swept me off,

The dancing rings of Mycalessus

Keep quiet. The man is raving.

The world of gods, their dancing footsteps beating out of time.

Dactylic hexameter: a moment where divine will is self-evident.

Concordantiae, dreams of humanity: what plans are they mapping?

Extra naturam,
Lūx,
Οκώσπερ τόξου τε και λύρης,[1]
Nuanced,

My vocabulary of emotions,
Incomplete account of reality,
Supersedes the connection

It is mostly like be part of the mystery I am trying to solve,
My apparatus, entangled material,
Meaningless to your ears

My words are gestures ceaselessly passing by,
Cutting the air without significance,
Scent whispering low
Nonetheless, defending themselves, must be voiced
That grand array of linking phonemes dashes and springs in agony
Striving is a limited action, a solipsistic glory
When measured in relation to the fixed crux
It is only a subordinate point of a view conceived in my imagination

Thus, making myself comprehensible is abandoned.

Ipse dixit: symbolic interactions

Diaphanous relevance: the charter theory of obscurity, in line with its ethos in order to move beyond the complete coincidental.

1 Like that of the bow and of the harp. Reference: Heraclitus of Ephesus, *On the Universe*.

Entailed

Castianira and Laothoe

Blameless we were

Married far from our homes

Me, Castianira, beautiful like the full-blown poppies when they burst
into red bloom north of the Scamander River.

Me, Laothoe, daughter of the Lelegian king, now walking among the
branches in Priam's orchard, watching the heavy clouds in the
merciless horizon.

Only the holy fire in the heavens could see our commitment in the
collective.

Political, oneiric, textual

With regard to the question of suggesting

Not surprisingly

There is nonlocality

There is no claim

We are product of two separate conditions and yet, there is no
    controversy

Available now in incomplete description

Simple

Complementarity

Simple

Apprehensiveness

Traces of our enfolding, memories

We are entailed exclusions.

Allowed

Chryseis

Experiencing a flower

The thousand petals and its pistils

Coming out of its roots and stems; dazzling aroma, luminous green

Plant-life on wild and barren stocks

Not a beginning nor an end

Unequal shining,

Utterance of a hymn

Ceremonial sunrise.

Proclamation.

(Because the chrysanthemum knew that those whose folly is greater

and more complete
they have claw-like hands, which they keep concealed at first.)

Chryseis formed an object of exchange
And no one was willing to answer her objections

Unpretentiously: probably there is a certain pleasure in rarities.
Fleeing voice, the golden one, milky skin and so young.

Unmixed libations: until mourning be turned to mirth.
Various forms of input: treble, alto and bass or perhaps the speaking
    raven, the dreadful dragon and Persephone.

Sorrow,
Fruitless air
Empty in her heart
The seeds of silkworms
Strings of light in her bare arms

The breath of the west wind
Stirred the right to something new:
A connection, a grounding conception; changing interests and
    concerns
She felt perfectly related, complied without being dissociated

Not instrumental although theatrical
Coercive power: a possible strategy of equilibrium

Sameness,
I think, a pleasurable artifice
Joined together,
Privileging

Allowed or banned?
The crucial finding: cultural transmission as a cumulative process
Practical reasoning
Justifying considerations
Legitimating the narrative:
'The remainder entitled to them by the principle of justice in
    acquisition and transfer.'
Chryses rejoicing, received his dear child.

Resisted

Chrysothemis

One of three daughters
No bride-price asked
An offer, a dowry to a man she never met
A denied offer, a dowry to a man, he never met her
That was all spoken about her name

Still, we know the names of her sisters,
Iphianassa filled Iphigeneia
Laodice filled Electra
Her sisters were in the spotlight. The precondition and the
    aftermath.

Her? A pale figure, a backwards send message, a return. Perhaps
　　also a permission.

No one was judged by Chrysothemis.

A paradox considering her name. Law of the gold, golden law, gold
　　as the law?

Her father's name? Her mother's name?

We know that, alright.

The brisk commands,

A weasel skin,

A fleet; Iphigeneia never to come back

A mission undertaken; Electra seized by rage

And yet Chrysothemis left behind, accepting her loneliness: a full
　　round moon gleaming over the mountain's slopes near her empty
　　natal home.

Forgotten by fate's storm-torn sea. Forgotten by the rushing
　　darkness over her home foothills. Forgotten by death's squads
　　crashing down her beloveds.

She needed no courage. She needed no praise.

The perished family,

A mark on a stone.

Stretching hands to the gods,

Every feature, her eyes and voice, sang life's vibrant music.

The spirit inside her never shrunk,

A small bird breaking through the pounding waves in the land of the
    dead, land engulfed in haze and night.
Pure gaze, bright sea, bathing in hope, no weeping tears
A silver atom, never concrete, stepping outward, resisting suffering
Holding tight the open sense of futurity
May I call her a starting place?

Entangled

Cleopatra Halcyon

Remember her?

That great beauty?

Meleager's bride.

What was her entanglement?

Personally, I think she was distinct in her mutuality

An individual element in Homer's poem about Ilium

In the world of gold masks, the daughter of Marpessa, Apollo's
 pursued loving maiden, without a drive on her own? I doubt.

Did her biology frame a constrained condition?

I mean, Meleager reveals himself as the denial of the warrior's
 pattern

The not-willing-to-fight warrior

Not willing to reassert the rationality of the others

Suspended by anger?

Suspended in the interim of his fantasies not marked by the exterior?

While Alcyone begs him to regain his natural position, his crucial
features:

The warrior's assumption to fight.

Halcyon and Meleager entail each other

Enfolding, reconfiguring, acting on the dynamic of possibility

He saved them all from the fatal day

His feelings?

Too late.

A deadly fascination.

A corpse among corpses.

Already a relic to his mother's murderous tears, her structural
relation of power and kinship.

There is no neutral device for observation

I am not sure how the Halcyon's fear of Curetes mounting the towers
of her home town and Meleager's mother, Althaea's lethal cry
'kill my son' contest in the symbolic terrain.

Profound implications locked on the crucial aspect.

The relic

An alterity from her son to the object to be extinguished

Separability and alterity

A brittle star

The crying Halcyon, permeated through and through acting as a
prism

In her own skin a sea bird

His mother's performance; the sedimenting practice.

The body located into the objective referent to be erased when it is
not initiated.

A state not detected, not a replacement but a change pointing into a
physical reality

Attached in a remarkable result: a mimetic imitation of a piece of
burning wood.

Evoked

Clymene

There is something with memory; it breaks down to very small molecules. It takes a swift gallop in the fissure of the moment, grows inside the body's nerves to finally escape as a minor modification in the breathing-time.

I belong to the breathing time
Eyes wide,
Heartbreaking
Words,
Clear as cicadas,
Gentle

Helen and her terrible beauty:

'There was a world,

'There was a treachery,

'There was a ring around you,

'There was two lambs and wine,'

That's all she said.

A fall in silence

Silence ends the agony

Forlorn in a continual guiding theme

'The object, the scene, the danger, were powerful incentives'

A thought wave, an admission to mortality

Predetermined reaction: waiting till the ground became firm enough

Predetermined reaction: resisting to acquired ideas

Evoked an inherent necessity; the human life

The sensuous impressions were not pronounced

Resultant:

Fleeting time, light passing through my fingers, Clymene, with her
    eyes wide open

Arises as a sort of reciprocal action

The moment unsightly reduced to inanimate mass

(Every modification in the reality become *ipso facto* a modifying
    principle)

Attracted by a verse such as the 'continuance of enduring thought'[1]
  or by the uncertainty itself

The closed curve of time was treated-not, for inaccessibility is an
  anxious bliss

'But you my child,' Helen said

'Greet the prospects which the future holds out; an error can be
  repaired.'

A reverent silence

A quiet nod

A sharp glance

Clymene, with her eyes wide open sees the rippling wave, the
  flowing time, the lonely flower of sorrow and triumph as it
  springs in a blazing speed, smashing the wind, reaching so high
  as if a black eagle flies the sky over the city's palisade scooping
  the weeping hearts with his fierce thrusting beak, breaching
  the steep walls, brimming the years to come with the unborn
  generations while scattering Troy's armies to the distant seas.

1 Lord Byron, *Manfred*, 1834.

Staged

Clytemnestra

I raised a platform and I staged a scene.

My wicked sister Helen. My treacherous sister Helen. I was hating
    her since we were children. My envy. Her beauty. Her divine
    beauty. My envy. Her fate. Her glorious fate.

The killing of my first husband Tantalus, the killing of my infant son.

My abduction, my forced marriage to Agamemnon, my sacrificed
    daughter Iphigenia.

My need for Aegisthus.

Trapped in a cloth net I stabbed Agamemnon.

I am a ghost now.

The staging scene has absorbed me. I repeat my words endlessly.

Learning through suffering?

Helen. She never suffered. My tremendously beautiful sister.
Menelaus couldn't resist her beauty.

Demanding for retributive justice I prompted an unusual interlude:
my fatal wound.

All my life turned out to be unexpectedness and aimless movement.
Establishing a personal claim on her own behalf.

But then it is well known when a woman calls her misfortune god too
works with her.

Restaging

Cassandra was collateral damage. Open strands of the crisis.

I led my daughter from Argos to Aulis. A bride of death.

Cassandra had the ability to suspend time. Ability to foretell the
future. She had to run. Instead, she has frozen into my will or
perhaps into the house's bloody history. I think she belongs in a
larger system of associations. Perhaps that of a double meaning.

'A drop of saffron-dyed blood has run to my heart.'[1]

Iphigenia and Cassandra as sacrificial animals. Their voices
restrained by a bridle.

Restaging

'And if I flee to Argos, they will come and seize the land and utterly
destroy it along with the Cyclopean walls themselves.'[2]

The army's impatience.

The construction of the oracle.

A set of alternatives: The crux of mental context.

Restaging

I was both a victim and a perpetrator although I never reversed from
good fortune to bad. Agamemnon was the agent of my misfortune
from the beginning.

Some asked for my motive and intent: What was I thinking?

Blood pollution persists until the crime is finally avenged. That was
my ethics.

Restaging

'The blood, dark spray of a salt and deathly dew, gushed and spouted
like raindrops on a parched field at the bursting of the bud.'

The fierce ancient avenger; what an orgasmic joy.

The House of Atreus as alterity within the self.

The space that wrecked our abode.

Restaging

Now I was a hateful raven. A woman abandoned by her husband. A
terrible evil.

Let's speak the dialect of Parnassus: A wedding rite, a torchlight
procession. The groom dead. I killed him. My robe, my net, my
blanket, my tapestry, my lover. All covered by death's promise. I
wear the crown of sorrow.

Agamemnon has insulted me.

Agamemnon the killer of the melodious nightingale.

Agamemnon walked on the purple drapery.

The Furies tracked him down or perhaps was my fury?

Restaging

Dreams wandering in the daylight.

All things pay retribution for their injustice one to another.[3]

The law of Time.

Ilion's citadel is fallen.

Long wastes of wind, held ship and unventured sea.

Restaging

Workings of hate, the storm of my dark thoughts.

The yoke of must-happen.

The tower of watch.

Helen: Noise of shield and sword

Iphigenia: Tears in mine eyes

Thus, I became a transitional figure, on the threshold between the
dead and the living.

Restaging

The songless song. Unintelligible sound.

The House of Atreus: Brides and victims

The speaking signs.

'A woman's eye that was soft, like misty rain,

'A flower which ate a man's heart with pity.

'But old sin loves, when comes the hour again, to bring forth new.'[4]

Restaging

A shining wind out of this dark shall blow

Above the eternal tide of tears

A beaming star

The resurrection of the dead: Manifestation of the subconscious.

1 Reference: Iphigenia in Aulis Euripides.

2 Reference: Aeschylus, *Agamemnon*.

3 Reference: Anaximander.

4 Reference: Aeschylus, *Agamemnon*.

Reenacted

Danae

Untangling fragments of my past:

Was a beautiful day when my father decided to lock me in his tower
(canopies drawn down firmly in my bedroom)

Since then, the sun scares me; the moon is my only friend (denying
words and prayers)

I can see the night sky; the roof is open (angry clouds menace my
psyche)

The rain falls inside (wild tears)

I live in this pit hole (I am not allowed to leave)

Preparing myself for death

Thus, I suppose, I try to forget how beautiful was the day before I found myself in the bronze well (fading dreams, door locked)

The uninvited prophecy
The secluded space
The impregnable tower
And yet,
Beams of golden light, like gems in a shining drapery, enclothe my
nights. Embrace my naked body. Cover my fall in the abysmal
space. Golden doves experienced as a divine cosmos. The moon
wraps my skin in a gleaming mantle. The stars lurk in hope for my
fallen realm. I, so lonely as an ideal dissolved into the darkness's
heart.

The invisible world predicted regal death
Attributing the reenactment to my child (magical produce of my
body)
Perseus (Phanebalos)
'Sleep, babe, and sea, be still'

He now departs:
Graeae
Stygian Nymphs
Slaying Medusa

Shielding reflections

Kohut's restoration of the self (narcissistic mirror transference)

Visual attraction; freezing gaze, flinty impetus, stony paralysis, congealed wastes

Neutralisation; loss of fruitful seductiveness, loss of prominent sexuality, loss of menacing rapprochement

(The outcome of a battle prompted by glacial conquest.)

Ketos: aggression, subjugation, exclusion

Disparagement: dominance of femininity

Andromeda: a threat

Is my son an identity theft or a gender saviour?

Residing greatly in symbols thus making himself immortal?

What about Andromeda?

All she was, a spiritual transgression?

In my opinion,

Perseus and Andromeda are mingled in equal and harmonious proportions;

A large organic canvas;

Incarnated bios

Icon stasis: Medusa carefully exposed as the castrated maternal genitals on Athena's aegis

(Freud's predominant regulation. I suppose, like my father, he

was powerfully absent perhaps he had also the allure of a god.
Displaying little interest on Andromeda's name and future.)

Mythmakers described my journey downwards
Forgetting that I know how to walk through their loci,
Their spatial map; my return
(Celestial yet rooted; not any longer a failed female)
Exposed at and by starlight
I sculpted myself deep into the real
Recreating my presence as free and yet regular influx of imagery
Restored myself forsaking the nebular hypothesis
Pursuing a bright living
Calm like a frivolous constellation

(Luxurious in azure
Avowed in vermillion
Mixed in green
Amazed in storming gold
Loved in lightning warmth)

Prolific in my innate force

Hushed

Diomede and Iphis

Two islands. Lesbos and Skyros.
Two lost, abducted daughters. Diomede and Iphis.
Two lovers. Achilles and Patroclus

Captivated: Bereaved families
Seduced: insinuating description
Hushed waft: without violence

Ferns and shrubs under a feverish sky
'Watch the new moon brilliant Achilles,' Phoenix son of Amyntor
said. 'Killing energy, accompanied by irritation. A sum of

personal situations. Agglomeration: Subversion, Insolence, Conceit.'

Brandishing an ordinary perception, adumbrating the use of logical adaptation, conserving the expression, distinguishing himself: Achilles turns away the embassy of Ajax and Odysseus. Phoenix stays, presenting an offer of reconciliation.

Reflecting on the fact that both Diomede and Iphis were sleeping on fleeces, woollen throws and soft linen sheets (not that we know anything about their dreams). Comparing, even unintentionally, a similar system of juxtapositions without changing the nature of the scheme, we can conclude at the following assertions:

a) There is implosion and reconfiguration

b) There is immediate consciousness: no fractures, safe ground

c) There is the determination of the imaginative faculty and the volatility of its efficient cause

Iphis waking up said: 'Infinitude is none other than one's own relation to self.'

Diomede declared: 'What a mighty spirit.'

Both laughed.

(Such was the polished yoke that kept both beasts apart)

Labelled

Eriopis

Bleak rays

Medon's banishment, wrath upon hushed earth

Ajax's death, thrust upon sharp rocks

La miserable coeur est trop faible pour me supporter

I was a mother and stepmother

They labelled me so cruel as being moulded from serpents

Such a difficult air to breath

Such a terrible accusation

Violent error, my son

Scattered leaves, my stepson

Why do I get the blame?

Absorbing the responsibility
(An averse and perilous path)
Shambling hooves of loneliness
A shift in pessimism that overemphasises the heed of a brutal taste
Savagery; dealing with others
Experiences lost in time; inside themselves (in their own
    experiencing space)

I was left alone
(In the reflective awareness of a lonely tree)
To love my fears
Achieving only a fractious dispute of the inescapable importance
    within myself
To love my life
Achieving to leave behind both mockery and humiliation
Achieving to be attached to myself
Self-preservation was my response
A perfectly real (neural) process

Engendered

Europa

The primal myth for displacement disguised as the discrepancy of gazes or as a pastoral idyll taking place in a bed of anemones somewhere in Crete.

1st Frame:

My glorious sons:

The underworld judges (Names: Minos, Rhadamanthus, and Sarpedon.)

My gifts:

The necklace (Charms: Laelaps, Javelin, Talos).

All things pay retribution for their injustice one to another.

My appellation:

Demeter Europa (Title: The daughter of Sidon. Description: The
broad-faced moon.)

My flowers:

Pearly, arranged beautifully in my golden basket.

The bull:

White. Dazzling white.

The horns:

Enticed by a pair of gilded blades. An ard plough.

The hooves:

Skimmed the waves, descending upon the darkening waters. A
bulbous bow.

The thiasos:

A marriage song played across time by conch shells.

The Shades:

'Does an empty image leading out from the ivory gate, play with me?'

2nd Frame:

Across the sea to Crete:

Melancholy, lack and pain.

Eschatology:

The dream is deceiving. The dream will come true.

Repetition:

Pasiphae in a wooden caw. Analogy to the Trojan Horse.

Sublimation:

The living body within. The beast-god. The continent to be.

Affiliation:

The bull piercers, blown into tempests, modulate the historical.

Metamorphosis:

An enigmatic marriage. Exposure to the indeterminate.

3rd Frame:

The clouds substance:

A purified heritage. Refined endowment. Sovereign power.

The crossover:

Transposed into the expansive gaze.

The matrimonial drink:

Cinnamon and balsam, frankincense and myrrh.

The sprinkles:

Sweet-smelling ambrosia.

The monument:

The unnamed continent identified.

The voice:

Clarifying or contemplating the towering mountains and the north
winds.

The image:

Self-disengaged and Imperial.

The mobility:

Assorted.

The Breaker:
Undisclosed.

4th Frame:

Phoenix (my father): Illustrative rebirth.

Telephassa (my mother): Essentially shining.

The legendary moment:

Attraction. Persuasion. Sense of a new selfhood. The variety of
forms. An articulated desire. Animal passion. Natural entity.
Biospheric. A foundation plunged into the impulse of a
flourishing attainment in unaccustomed form: The bull's hot
breath acting on percepts, assuming the conquest, fetishised by
a functioning assertion, replicated as steer power or economy,
reproduces its charging energy surviving materiality and despite
all constraints breaks through the imposed considerations
forcing his eyes glare forth into the glassed ebbing of the
unbounded cosmos.

Remodeled

Hecamede

When Machaon met me, he asked: 'Are you pleased with the
   outcome of your wish?'
Coming from a small island I always dreamed of distant places.
Did I wish to leave? Yes, but not as a captured woman.
'I wish,' I said to him, 'to travel in honour of my abilities.'
He agreed.
Now I am in the service of the old wise horse-man.
Machaon taught me how to prepare the Pramnian wine. A medicinal
   drink. Based on a special wine made from a unique vineyard
   mixed with pale honey and sparkled with white barley. It is served
   in an adequately exceptional cup. Two gold doves perched on

each handle. Heads bending to drink.

Travelling in their direction felt as if intruding on my own
personality.

A prevalent idea, old and fixed, reappearing and fading.

(*Avec un sourire timide*) Machaon said. 'It is really remarkable to get
integrated into your own imaginary life.'

'I reformed myself as an artistic idea,' I replied.

(Was the sentiment, I suppose, that was born due to this
extraordinary object)

His fatherly expression, his gentle gaze, his encouraging speech.

The unattainability of joy melted in his heart.

Remodelling and perfecting myself,

My propensity became transparent to me,

Binding us in a solemn and trusting oath.

Bestialised

Hecuba

In the face of extraneous forces.

Malignity of present and future.

Honey mellowed wine, the libation cup.

Ilion was ablaze.

I prepared the body of my grandson for burial.

My children lost.

Wept for the dead.

A moving principle: confused turmoil of hunger and hatred.

Incense.

The low places of eternal damnation.

Exaltation and defend.

The conquering prowess.

The instrumental relation to others.

Unrestricted reason.

Perhaps sitting still and doing nothing.

The barrier of moral conviction.

Private sentiments, my sentiments.

Maximisers.

Coercion in the name of interpretation.

Competing answers.

Sheer luck.

A grave wrong.

The arbitrary link: the limits of desert.

Ius ad bellum

Ius in bello

Uncertainty matters.

Did they meet the condition?

A pre-established procedure.

(Swallowed or rejected)

To have power is to have power over others.

Shifting gears for a moment: the sympathetic kindness.

Manipulation of the outcome.

Ferociousness.

War is inherently violent.

Their degree of branching and the extent to which the features at
successive scales are related is a perspective for existential survival.

Projected outward.

Unjust harm.

A form of consequentialism.

Counterintuitive implications.

The aftermath of the fall of Troy.

Successive calamities.

My voice rang out in tears.

A throbbing chant.

My silent body lying on the ground.

A barren salt sea.

The white bones.

Enslaved.

Bared foot.

Clothed in rags.

Bereaved.

An icon of tragedy.

They sacrificed my daughter.

They murdered my son.

Maternal grieving, *Mater Dolorosa*.

Mad upon seeing the corpses of my children.

Mad by sorrow.

A potent improbability: relieving the burden of grief by other grief.

Emotional intensity.

Catalysed thoroughly the violent action.

'No one should touch my child.'

I blinded the killer of my son transforming lament into revenge.
Then,
Physical detachment was conceptualised as retribution,
Mental states as aberrations.

Barking like a dog.
Me, a she-dog with fiery eyes.
(Burning eyes of heaven)

Animalisation: crushing the human.
Animalisation: the shattered city.

This was a drama with roots in societal relations. This was a drama of
    a dark fate. *Un ensemble représentatif.*
They said: and none of these things is not Zeus
I say: and none of these things is Zeus

Qualified

Helen

Appropriating the conversant: every story gets told.

The real, the fictitious and the fabulous,
With each moment a new condition of mind is set forth.

Two orders, the emancipated and the heralded
Both performing their roles, a symbiotic rehearsal.
Suddenly a subtle strain,
A territory; wild orchids in the purple sky
Trembling earth, unleashes her roar in a place that never before
    trampled into the dust

Mediated fragments; harbouring and preserving
Schematic restoration
Revealing the repetitive loneliness; a white blossom
Ebbs and flows; my presence in a fusing space
'Mes reveries moroses'
Or the unwillingness to state the effective expression
No, no; I do not wish to legitimise the emptiness
I prefer the botanical metaphor: rooted in heavens,
The stable centre,
The sun's inhabitation of the summer,
Inoffensive, amiable, delightful.

Il fait beau, si beau
Comme in feuille au vent ; je nage dans mes reves
Le ciel
Presque pur
Presque bleue
Je n'insiste pas
Je me tire par la melody
Aggradir mon regard, J'ai change.

Apparently,
A sense of growing meaning as the text is still imagined composing
 for itself a space augmented by emotion

Ensembles of conventions

Equipped for the moment of happiness

Strange, I always believed that happiness it is not captured by the
moment

Happiness was matter of resilience

The moment vanishes, collapsing into a sole point extremely low to
hold the expectation

I think, deploy my thoughts secures my effort.

Hidden markers

Accidental trivia

Aspire

The advancement to the field of lynxes; a cup filled with joy

An outstanding landmark; the looming Scaean Gates

Effectively we experience our own dream image

The serene presence of the sunlight

Admirable like a swan's flight over the rugged ramparts;

Helen cloaking herself once more in her husband's shimmering
linen calls herself his wife

Restoring her body as affiliation,

Gratifies her natal land with her beauty.

Juxtaposed

Hippodamia and Caenis

Abducted by the Centaurs, our guests, on my wedding day

What a terrible assault

Wasn't Cupid's arrows, it was Centaurs' impression of strength

Or, possibly, primitive parts of their brains activated through the
   roughest of the storms:

Genetic interest and breeding offspring

(Pity though that there is no evolutionary mechanism to inhibit rape
   and killing)

Later, when the war was over, I asked my husband if we dehumanised
   them or if it was solely their fault.

He said that we invited them to our wedding, although he admitted

that the wine was strong and they drank too much. But he was
certain, these human hybrids couldn't be anything else than
brutes.

During my abduction I felt like I was trying to keep hold of a broken
nag without reins

Nevertheless, I had a strong hold on my senses (after all I was the
inventor of the bridle's bit)

I felt also their hidden and ambitious motives.

Counter reckoning, you may say.

What depressed and dazzled circumstances

(Floating on the surface are depicted in metopes and it can be seen
both as forms of eloquence and carnage)

Centauromachy

My dear friend Caenis, who was transformed to the alpha male and
invulnerable warrior Caeneus during the fight was retransformed
to a bird, after he was crushed into chthonic by pine trunks.

Such a juxtaposition of insinuations,

Like entering and participating in a world of fiction or as if lilies
were mixed with violets

Amphitheatre spectators might fill by now a bit disoriented.

Caeneus transgenderism, for instance, might have been an anima
and animus dynamic with further inferences.

Was I, the horses' master, the victim of men that were half horses?

(As if we asked was Achilles the foster son of half-horse or half-beast
Chiron?)

What meant the invitation to our wedding? Was really without
purpose?

As a sign of radical changes or a piece of fate and loftiness of power

Active forces might turn reactive (occasionally)

Did exteriority, traits and genotype form an outgroup? A negative
identity?

Reorienting biases: it seems to me like an immense rodeo.

At the end of the day, I was the only winner:

The mother of Sarpedon and the tamer and defeater of the Centaurs.

Spared

Hypsipyle

Trim trim trap trap

Silly silly men

Only death do they deserve

Trim trim trap trap

Kill them, kill them fast

Trim trim trap trap

Vague and soft and pale and dull

No memory to peel the wood

Trim trim trap trap

Old battles

Trembling dust, bronzed pin

Cold corps

Count them, no one to cross

Kiss to kiss,

No one to miss

Send them all to the deep deepest pit hole

Laugh then ha ha ha

Climb then through the dusk

Throw them to the sea

Don't worry

We are fine

No grave

Nothing of their passing by

We are saved

And we saved our children's life

When the women of Lemnos killed all their men Hypsipyle saved
her father. Actually, the plan was his. The men had to die. An
infectious sexually transmitted disease. They had to do it. Her
father knew the outcome. He had seen it with his own eyes.
They spare no one. He only spared himself. As a king he had the
privilege to plot in advance his own rescue.

Performing one's social function: producing virtue through a crime?
Was it a rational decision?
No inner protest?

Were no competing voices?

Why Dante has Hypsipyle in Limbo?

There is faith in human progress, I suppose.

The fulfilment of Hypsipyle: Facilitator of her father's vision to
protect life through death.

At the end of the day, she saved him (or the constitution).

Accepting the values that were denied to all others,

Kept intact her reputation by ascribing both right and duty as her
own principles

Exhausted all understanding as a requirement to her status

While the rest of the women fell into the abyss of the inevitable
absence of humanity

Like monstrous misconfigured existences breaking into a choice of
destruction

Rejected

Without capability of being rational, exiled from culture

Denouncing ethical necessity

Killing the father

Killing the husband

Killing the lover

Suppressing the conflicting part

A daunting savagery?

Lack of compassion? Of affection?

Did they feel pain? Remorse? Guilt?

Did they feel misguided?

Disharmony, fear's compulsion

Murderesses

Thus, was necessary to remove Hypsipyle

Not to kill, not to execute

Killing was not any more an option

To remove and reestablish the lost city and the civil rules, reconcile
the past

Reaffirm life, reaffirm intimate relationships, fathers, partners,
lovers

Engaging in the normative

Pronouncing life's alleged right to ethos as social acceptance

The moral imperative: of not exalting oneself above others.

Cancelled

Laodice

The breaking of the waves in the small pebbles at the seashore
The beauty breathed
The flight of the seabirds
The light in the deep meadows
The green besides the sands
The shining peace

And yet,
A growing web
Dark red
Fills the air

Races the wind
Blazes iron chains
(Craving to ruthless killing each other)
Surges and rambles against any sense of rationality

And yet,
Hauls and sways, commands and tactics, spies and armies
They all have been swallowed up in a chasm that opened on the earth
(The whole campaign cancelled while negotiations started
or so I wished)

Frightened

Medicaste

Death scares me. Living scares me too.

What might happen to us over and above our wanting and doing
scares me the most.

Everything around me seems aggressive or potentially aggressive.

Edgy. Sharp. Racked.

The slightest communication, the slightest contact, might turn into
horror.

(I am not getting out of home anymore)

Do you call it agoraphobia?

Bend your heads and see.

My heart is torn.

We are lethal to each other. Every minute.

Anger and sorrow are mounding our souls complying to this
dreadful folly,

Thrashing glories and shames

Knocking teeth

My nights charged with loneliness fluctuate into a slinking dark

Sweeping away feelings

Refusing beauty

Erasing hope

My husband's arm around my waist. Craving. I miss his arms.

Clear, warm water. Showering me with kindness. His gentle love.

Now, a dead corpse. I mourn him. I mourn my life.

Trained

Myrina

Lemnos

As I was walking in the fields of Lemnos, I saw those beautiful
flowers. Orange—almost red. It was a rare moment of happiness
in a foreign place. Grasslands, savannas and high mountains
covered with deep green pine trees was my homeland. I was never
fond of the sea. Especially after the vanishing of the Atlanteans.

Atlanteans

I never conquered their gorgeous city. To do what in a city? I am
not fond of their closed limited spaces. But I saw them sink to
their deaths. I watched them from my crowning mountain. An
earthquake created an immense uproar, a vortex, as if the tartars

of the sea's depths opened. The sea that you call Caspian. And
they were all of them sucked in as through a hole. Caspian Sea
was double the size you know, perhaps even bigger. I can't tell
with certainty. A great bulk of water. In the delta of the restless
river that poured his waters in this deep dark sea started a
great construction of channels and streets and floating houses.
Atlantis. Erected on little ground and much water. Like Venice.
Just to give an example. The city was constructed as rings of
compartments and channels around a piece of stable terrestrial
center. Nobody was able to conquer such a construction. I assure
you of that. Everything else are stories or unwillingly told lies.
The 'festival of roses'.

We never banished maternity. Our daughters were welcomed. Boys
were given to their fathers if they didn't die at birth. A congenital
defect. Most of our boys died. Young women from all the places
of the savanna were coming to join our tribe. We accepted only
the competent. Call it recruitment. Some wished to live free from
domestic tights. Others to defend themselves from rapes and
enslavement. They found discipline and the art of war. Our life
is beautiful but harsh. Men keep coming from distant places to
subjugate my tribe. We had to be proactive. We had to be ready.
We had to be skilled.

Lemnos

As I said, I was happy riding the fields of Lemnos. I felt welcomed.
Wearing my bronze armature with golden stripes the Lemnian

women called me Artemis daughter.

I said to them: I worship women. I worship you.

They fell in ecstasy. Thrilled.

They named their city after me. Myrina. Google it if you don't believe me.

The majority of men were absent. Sailors. Only young boys and old men, left behind, working in the yellow straw fields. The fields I was galloping on my beautiful black horse.

Attachment

Love was not a prohibited action. Why would you say so? We loved our daughters. We loved each other. We loved our freedom. We loved our horses. We loved our lands. Do I have to continue?

We were female warriors. We couldn't sustain a household. We had to run an army. A tribal army.

Accused

Our world was open and vast. We were part of the nature's strong hold. Vibrating a totality. Intertwined in an absolute state of fiery identification of primal energy and self. And yet, our discipline, our rules, our training had nothing bestial nor animalistic. We dominated our lives and our horses.

Sexually charged

The Amazonian brawler. The conflation. The intensification.
An image, strong as an impulse. It is not the fortress to be conquered. It is not the flower to be deflowered. It is the flight to be annihilated. It is the woman to be tamed. It is the danger

132

to be confronted. It is the penetrating victory of an arrow or a spear curved into a fascinating body. It is not the stirring taste of hunting; it is the thirsty agony of meeting. The challenge of the wondrous opponent. Wrestling is also sexually charged. In different way, the body sweats. Uttering a performable union. The Amazon fires up the air. Energising the instinct of an unfathomed union. Unachievable at the same time.

Legend

I love Kleist's work on Penthesilea. I love it so much that I wish to rewrite it.

Collapsed

Niobe

The Weeping Rock

On the lonely mountain slopes

Time and again, perished and destroyed

Hubris

Punishment

Execution

Suffering

Alteration

Disillusionment

A structure based on centuries of past consecrated to death.

Worn to the bone, lost in crags, flooding of grief and tears,

Warned them,

The funeral took place on camera,

While the rain poured down on her face and the thundering sky run
over the clouds

She was the unusual subject

An open conversation among humans and gods

She was a stonified horror

Remarkable in its ordeal

A warfare mountain

Bent

Unwillingly coerced

A sun cut, dark against morning light

A contractarian seeks, the product of self-imposition

The approach of ostentation, a deterrence against the conceit,

Deprived of pride

Available to the winds

Collapsed forever to a gravestone

'Pause, my heart. Hidden in stone and earth my beautiful children
are.

'I too have turned into stone with sorrow

'I am dying

'For my soul is broken

'My breath has flown away

'And all that is left from my heart, a glaring surface'

Lifted

Phrontis

Panthous arms are empty
Euphorbus dropping back
The red-haired captain rips his sweet life away

Wreaked words. Aching heart.
Lovely Phrontis. Floating beauty divided by ideas and impressions
She attempted to push her own soul out of herself

Euphorbus locks splashed with blood
Intensive as any other physicality
A strange immediacy of the presented sight

Elicited from the primary fact: nothing to remain

Relatedness, bestrode the perishing, sealing the scarce
Togetherness, an ideal endlessness

A unique experience
Trembling feelings repeating dread and cold
Deep-set piercing eyes, insightful approach
Bearing, to mask and fuse reality
She refused; the world went black
An entire plain
Flood
Killer tides
Pounding waves
Clouds of crows
Passing by, she rises without future, a waving past
Although definitions of thoughts conceived in the regard of self-
    preservation
Recreated the impulse to realise herself through the frozen sky, on
    the mountain ice, in the glassy sea, within the crackling moment
A last look upon existence:
A basket of grapes, few flowers, to see the morning light, a reflection
    in the shining blue, a necklace, the arms of her sons, loaves of
    bread, a final gesture, expectation, wide-spread wings, sleep, the
    endless night.

Phrontis solitary and confident steps lifted her shade far from earthly
things.

Dismayed

Polydora and Phylomedusa

Compelling cases

(Writing about them)

Allusion

(And) mere trifles

Some variations

I have nothing in particular to say

Nothing to mould or fashion

The design and execution: no adequate information

Illustrative matter: derived as quasi-impersonations

A gloss: prominent figures (elaborating puppets)

Having existed as wives and mothers and yet
Sensed as
Limited dimensions, common formulas and prudish shades
(Notable lack of concern from my side)

Finding a signification or purchasing a circumstantial statement
Perhaps writing down a remark such as 'how much truth it contains a
    line that has lost the point of departure.'

Saturation and failure.
Upwards or downwards
Owned or disowned
Brevity or exaggeration
I need an attitude to defend
(Or I will dismay any further attempt to continue my narration)

The tables are turned. The images infused. My reiterated assertion.
    Aggravation.
I have just admitted: Chaos is not a theory.
Multifariously (Endeavoring to dictate an obvious consideration or
    dramatised passage for later refinement.)

Portrayed

Polymela

A *pas de deux*.

His self-controlled movement, his attentiveness, his steps. A
virtuoso. I was dancing with Hermes. Wearing my long dress
shaped by the night's breeze in swarming ripples folding one in
the top of the other like tiny soft sea waves under a shining wind.
Holding krotala in my fingers. My arms raised up. Portraying a
rectangular shape.

Young girls, sweet maidens, danced around us. Lightly leaping and
clapping their hands. They wore saffron garments. Looking like
bridal veils or bearskins. My instructor stood near the seashore.

Sand dunes and pine trees. Her dress embroidered with golden thread. Bees, griffins and fawns. A pair of girls, imitating the birds, danced sinking down and again springing up on their haunches. A chariot drawn by a deer rested behind them. A choral ensemble was weaving a lovely hymn filling the night's gown with its beauty. My heart melted as melts the rare spring snow under sun's rays.

We had a hut covered by a delightful prairie rose. My father cultivated a piece of land. A stunning vineyard. I spend my summer at the beach. Waiting for this incomparably unique night. Practising my dances every afternoon with the aid of my instructor. Such a beautiful summer.

I was gathering fresh rose petals in my dress when the swift arrow of Eros fallen in my tender heart. Romance started when Hermes looked upon me. Singing the maiden song by hitting two seashells to keep the rhythm. He was walking near the peaceful sea, naked. His enchanting power. Lifted my heart to the Olympian sky.

The star-child of the dancing midnight, my son Eudoros, was a demigod.

Rescued

Theano

Parallel approaches

Potentiality or conformity?

Perhaps the deployment phase

Performed (repetitive although depending on many factors)

Proper combination

Loosely inspired

Activated while addressed

Challenge:

Shallow modelling (as usually an arrow represents a connection)

History: shifts, scales and rotates,

Elementary features: Gibb's state
Sudden observation: mineralogical, petrographic, permeable

For Theano all was a simple flash
Blessed as she was with the darkness; an owl of the night
Rescued with glorious gifts; veering past and deathless fate
Shimmered in the sun on golden settles; as she dashed on the
    vaulting sky her grey eyes

Here is her message:
The ocean's magnificence
lithe breaking up from the broad earth
quivering into the air seaweed and glistening fish
flows across the earth
standing fast, rules the world
into the offering light of day
gulping down monuments and signs
marvels and offerings
contingents and flags
luring them all to ruin
dissolving them all to nothingness
(the whole world hanging in the mid-air)

Theano was never rigid or unrelenting
Thrilled and marvelled she sees the steep heights, the looping cable

rounding their horns.

'Tell me,' she asks the old horseman. 'Will they give me my rightful
share?'

'Indeed,' he said. 'Let me offer you this honoured armour and my
winged sceptre.'

A towering fir tree and the immortals bird watching,
Bronze Throat; a Nighthawk

'Wait, please my heart. That's what I propose: the fluttering dove.'

Epimyth

A passageway

Winter

A flame blew green and blue

Behind two stars that shine not

Revealed a line so dark as the winter's daring sky over the snow's
parching day

Unease made from silk

Anew awakening winds

News, reports and media across the world comprehended the
relevance only by means of speculation

A memory stronger than human power fuelled the question

Illuminating the discovered by identifying its manner to be:

Our distant roots, those that left behind by the meanness of the
circumstances

Northerly winds of sparse rain unreasonably renounced reflection,

   perception, assertion

Regarding

Ideals and Myths

No one provides a comprehensive view and yet everybody will see

   the geometry replaced

The woman feels, the girl asks

How a pillar might be removed without falling the edifice?

Past and Future connected, a sign is a sign of emphasis

And yet, 'These things were all so, but setting in of the cold was not

   much out of season.'[1]

So really reassuring to read that the prevailing winds never

   proved fatal.

1 Reference: Hippocrates of the Epidemics, Book I.

Peaceful Morning

Gripping dreams in the deep caverns of the blue
Small voices from firs and algae, twigs of olive trees and sunbeams
But the jaws of wrath are threatening the moonlit night.

'Another war without glory and another peace without quiet'[1]

Not anymore

No one will be allowed to bleed the beauty of the landscape

A black ship as night, banner heavenly blue, wrapped in a cloud,
Penetrating each front, smashing all lines, flushes a sharp warning

   and message,

(The impending superstructure; a protruding shield)

Watches and wards, protecting for all times the peaceful morning.

1 Reference: Ezra Pound, *The Cantos,* 1962.

Acknowledgements

I would like to express my gratitude to the British Council and Kingston Writing School for supporting the writing of this book.

For the wonderful work on this book, I am very thankful to the MA students Rachel Cotton, Ida Langeland Hagen, Rebecca Hampstead, Priti Sundaram Mudaliar and the Course Leader Emma Tait.

I am deeply grateful to Dr. David Rogers, as I always will be, for his generous support.

About the Author

Athena Gaga, MSc candidate, MA, BEng, is the author of Mehen, the Oracle and the Time Movers, published by Kingston University Press in 2019. She worked as a senior designer in the telecommunications sector in Greece and abroad. And, later on, as a teacher in public high schools in Greece. Two of her stories appeared in the collected writings from the Kingston Writing School and the British Council International Creative Writing Summer School in 2016 and 2018. She lives in the present day in Ioannina, Greece with her son, a young adult with special needs, and her parents.

About Kingston University Press

Kingston University Press (@KU_press) has been publishing high-quality commercial and academic titles for nearly fifteen years. Our list has always reflected the diverse nature of the student and academic bodies at the university in ways that are designed to impact on debate, to hear new voices, to generate mutual understanding and to complement the values to which the university is committed.

Since 2017 all the books we have published have been produced by students on the MA Publishing and BA Publishing courses, bringing to life a range of community and creative projects, often partnering with organisations from our local community or poets from the university's vibrant writing community. While keeping true to our original mission, and maintaining our wide-ranging backlist titles, our most recent publishing focuses on bringing to the fore voices that reflect and appeal to our community at the university as well as the wider reading community of readers and writers in Kingston, the UK and beyond.